The Minimalist Vegan

A simple manifesto on why to live with less stuff and

more compassion

By Michael & Maša Ofei

"Art is theft." —Pablo Picasso

Uncopyright

All of the ideas in this book are borrowed therefore do whatever you like with the content. All that we ask is that you continue to spread ideas about simplicity and compassion in a way that works for you.

Published December 2017 by Minimalist Company Pty, Limited, written by Maša and Michael Ofei, edited and researched by Melanie Bertaud, and cover design by Karolis Zukas.

ISBN: 978-0-6482410-9-6

"It's not because things are difficult that we dare not venture. It's because we dare not venture that they are difficult." ~ Seneca The Younger

CONTENTS

INTRODUCTION

We live in a world of bigger, faster, more. Bigger portions, faster cars, more clothes. More social media, more television, more stuff. But "more" doesn't mean "better."

On a global scale, this unrestrained consumerism has given rise to a frightening environmental crisis, the brutal slaughter and mistreatment of animals, an epidemic of physical and mental health issues, and an economic system teetering on the brink of collapse. The happiness that adverts promise never materializes once we take that shiny new item home, yet we work every waking hour to buy it or buy it on credit. We are sadder, fatter, and more stressed than ever before.

The way we live our lives needs to change.

Two lifestyle concepts can free us from the shackles of consumerism: Minimalism and veganism.

Brought together, they provide a compelling solution to the modern-day slavery of always wanting more. Through mindful choices, we can reconnect with a conscious, meaningful way of life.

HOW TO READ THIS BOOK

The Minimalist Vegan is less of a *how*-to book and more of a *why*-to book. A manifesto on why to live with less stuff and with more compassion.

We hope that by the end of it, you'll have the thirst and passion to architect your life in a way that brings you purpose and joy every day.

We respect your time and understand that you have competing interests. That's why we've written this to be read within a few hours. Yes, even if you'd consider yourself to be a slow reader!

Each chapter can be read independently, so feel free to jump ahead to a section that resonates with you. That said, reading the book from start to finish is a great way to build momentum as you manifest your ideas and dive into strengthening your values or shifting your mindset to start a fulfilling journey.

MINIMALISM MEETS VEGANISM

In recent times minimalism has become a trend, even though it's a concept that has been around for centuries. It's all over mainstream media, and we've seen it used across various industries including fashion, design, food, technology, beauty, housing, and more. We even named our company Minimalist Company Proprietary Limited! But when the hype-dust clears, what does minimalism actually mean?

Minimalism has traditionally been linked to pure, intentional art and design concepts. But we believe it's much more than that. We define minimalism as the process of identifying what is essential in your life and eliminating the rest. Less is more.

Our modern lifestyles are far from minimalist. With so many distractions around us, we often find it difficult to create time and space to enjoy the simple things in life, like spending time with our loved ones, exercising, getting creative, cooking, or just doing nothing. We're too busy being overwhelmed by physical, digital and mental clutter that leads to increased anxiety and an overall sense of dissatisfaction. Minimalism is an antidote to that state of overload.

We're passionate about ruthlessly simplifying. However, we feel that the minimalist concept has room for improvement. In fact, it can be enhanced with the addition of vegan principles. Minimalism is, at its core, anti-consumerist, and can be a way of showcasing "purchasing power," or in this case "non-purchasing power." Veganism can be used in the same way. In many aspects, both ideals look toward the same goal: being conscious of exploitative and wasteful practices to protect our health, the environment, and the lives affected by unrestrained consumerism (whether human or animal).

Imagine a world where food and products are made ethically and in a way that supports our planet's ecosystems. Imagine a world where we are no longer spending all our time and energy accumulating things we don't need or can't afford.

The combination of these two ideals has the power to shift the demand for what we consume dramatically. That's why we work hard every day to live a minimalist, vegan lifestyle. It's not perfect, and we don't always get it right, but we believe it's an ideal worth pursuing.

While veganism and minimalism are unique in their own right, they work together beautifully. The underlying theme that links the two concepts together is mindfulness: being mindful of what you consume, whether food or luxury goods. It's about being aware of how every decision you make impacts you and what's around you. For example, a minimalist vegan is not only selective about how many things they buy, but they're also careful about how those things were sourced and made. Now you may be thinking, this sounds idealistic and even stressful, but when you're passionate about serving the world however you can, the effort becomes second nature.

Minimalism and veganism are perfectly complementary lifestyles that together have the power to spark positive global change. So, are you ready to embark on your minimalist vegan journey?

"THE MORE VIRUS"

When did we become a society dedicated to wanting more all the time? More gadgets, more cars, more space, more social media, more news, more clothes, more friends, more stuff. There's a virus in town. Something that we like to call "The More Virus".

Our world has been locked into a system of free-market capitalism for decades. We live in an economic system based on constant growth. In other words, a system that relies on us to consume more. Companies produce mountains of things that we do not need, and advertising campaigns convince us that we need those items to feel happy, fulfilled, joyful, desired, and worthy. Over $170 billion is spent globally every year just on digital advertising.[1] "The More Virus" has become stronger over the years as advertising budgets have increased. But you can rise above mass marketing, and live life on your own terms.

You've probably walked past a shop before and spotted something that you just *had* to have. We've all had those moments, but how often does this happen to you? Once a month? Once a week? Every day? And how have these desires impacted your life?

Why Do We Always Desire More?

Is it because we care too much about what others think of us? About their reaction when they come to our house or see us in that outfit? Are we trying to bandage insecurities about ourselves and our lives with retail therapy? Is it purely out of boredom or to fill a void? What triggers our desire for material possessions? Do we even really know?

According to Harvard Business School Professor Gerald Zaltman, 95% of our purchasing decisions are made subconsciously.[2] We buy based on our emotions, and then use logic to justify the purchase later. For example, you might walk past a coffee machine in a department store. Your subconscious has linked that particular product to a happy family scene, thanks to a television advert. On a subconscious level, you're craving the connection of a relationship, and that emotion is what will drive you to buy the item.[3],[4] Not the need to make your barista-style coffee every morning. You don't really need it, but you then justify it to yourself: "It looks great in the kitchen; I needed something to complement the food processor; I can finally host those dinner parties and impress my friends; I can save on take-out coffees; It wasn't that expensive after all."

Every day we are subjected to hundreds, if not thousands, of messages specifically designed to connect a positive emotional response to a product, with the aim of making you buy it. Bus stops, train platforms, television, the internet, magazines, newspapers, flyers, billboards, your phone, apps, your laptop, or your tablet.... Everywhere you look, there are adverts—many of them now "targeted" to your interests, based on what you search for online, even based on the conversations you have on social media. And these adverts encourage us to buy more by promising us that more stuff equals more happiness: And that is a lie.

Pursue Less

As you successfully pursue less of the non-essentials, you free up your capacity to spend quality time with loved ones, reading the book that's been sitting on your bedside table collecting dust for the last two years, trying a new hobby/venture, experimenting in the kitchen or exploring the world. You will spend less time wanting to accumulate stuff or trying to make or borrow money to buy things.

Have You Caught "The More Virus"?

There are many ways "The More Virus" appears in our lives. To see how present it is in yours, here are a few areas to analyze:

Work

You likely spend more time at work than anywhere else. With such a significant time commitment, it's crucial that you ask yourself: are you happy with the work that you do? Have you taken on more than you can handle? Are you striving too hard for something that's not even that fulfilling? Do you have three tedious part-time jobs just to meet your current lifestyle outputs? Unfortunately, many of us wake up every weekday dreading to go to work. That's not what life should be about, we should be excited or at least content about what we do.

Clothing

In this age of cheap and fast fashion, most of us have too many clothes—you are not alone. But how many of the clothes in your wardrobe do you wear? Do they all fit, or are you saving some for when you lose those ten pounds? Do some of them need altering? Is it worth it or would it be better to give it away? Do you need everything in your drawers or can you cut down the number of items you own so it's quality over quantity?Answering these questions will help you develop your own sense of style. You won't be so influenced by the latest trends, but more focused on what suits your figure.

Household Items

What's in your cupboards? Are they full of things you've brought home just because they were cheap or free? Are they overflowing with things that have been given to you, but that you have no real use for? Are you holding on to the second iron just in case you need a spare one? Does the item have a specific purpose or is it just filling the empty space next to the couch? Keep the things that bring you joy, but how much of that is real joy? It's okay to have empty spaces, not every corner or shelf needs to be filled.

Vehicles

Our planet could do with fewer cars on the road, and your budget will always benefit from cutting down on car costs. How many cars do you need? Could you use public transport, cycle or walk to work instead? How about carpooling? Do you have that second car purely for convenience or out of necessity? We have conditioned ourselves to always have everything available at our fingertips, this includes getting around quickly and easily. This doesn't always have to result in an extra vehicle.

Bills

Which of your recurring expenses are truly essential? Do you need the satellite TV contract and all three online on-demand movies subscriptions as well? Are two

memberships to online yoga programs genuinely helping you get more flexible? How often have you used
your gym pass? Remember that less is more in situations like this. Imagine the amount of money you'll
save just by looking at reoccurring expenses you don't
use.

Sports And Hobbies

Are you having fun, or are you participating out of a
sense of duty and fear of letting your teammates
down? Were you pressured into it because your best
friend wanted a cross-fit buddy, or do you genuinely
want to be there as well? Are there other things you
want to try but don't have the time because of these
and other commitments? Are you doing it out of guilt,
joy or fear? It's okay to be selfish and say no sometimes. You only have one life, really ask yourself what
you want to be doing with your spare time.

Digital Possessions

You know, the hundred apps you have on your phone, the thirty blog posts you have saved in your bookmarks folder, the countless tabs you have open at any given time on your computer, the ten podcasts you're listening to or the five hundred unread emails you have sitting in your inbox. We've all been there at some stage in our lives. Even these digital consumables accumulate in our hard-drives and our heads, creating mental clutter. Dealing with information overload can lead to your brain being wired all the time because you are always distracted or over-stimulated. This can end up disrupting your sleep, quality of life and your relationships.

Friends

As Jim Rohn famously said, "You are the average of the five people you spend the most time with." So, choose your friends wisely! Are you still friends with people from your childhood because you have things in common and enjoy each other's company, or only because you have known each other forever? Do your friends add value? Do you feel uplifted after you spend time with them, or do you leave every catch-up feeling unmotivated and confused about why you still have this person in your life?

By analyzing these areas of your life, you'll be able to see where there may be room for growth or change. These questions might make you feel a bit uncomfortable at first, but the relief that comes from beginning to free yourself of unnecessary stuff is so much more rewarding than holding onto something just because you are scared of change or letting go.

Free Yourself From The More Virus

Why do you want more? What's your trigger? Adverts get to work on many levels: they prey on our insecurities, our desire to belong, our need to connect, our longing for love. Get to know yourself. So in that impulsive purchase moment, you can be aware of what is pulling you to make that decision. This is powerful, because once you become aware of what you are craving—what you truly need to be happy—you'll be able to choose something that brings you happiness.

Brain scans reveal that our brains make a decision up to seven seconds before we are even aware of it.[5] So it takes time to change our patterns and behaviors, but keeping these questions in mind will arm you with the right mindset for positive change and make it easier in the future.

Guilt-Free Consuming and The Minimalist Antidote

Why do we buy things we don't need? Of course, there's a momentary high when we make that purchase. We want to reward or treat ourselves. Maybe we're bored, and shopping is a fun form of entertainment. Perhaps we feel entitled? We deserve it, and it's acceptable. Advertising gives us a helping hand in these perceptions. Many brands have caught onto the fact that guilt is dangerous to consumerism and now add reassuring strap-lines like "Don't worry, if you change your mind within 60 days you can bring it back" or "Money back guarantee if you find the same product cheaper." But realistically, how many of us take the item back or look around for the same product at a lower price point after purchasing?

Have we become a guilt-free consuming society? We know that if after a week, month or if it does take up too much room, it's okay: we can give it to charity, family or friends, or maybe even sell it. With more platforms where second-hand items can be sold, re-purposed or reused, we have an extra excuse to carry on with our compulsive buying habits, guilt-free. Someone else can make use of it later, right? That's the mentality.

However, mindless consuming isn't guilt-free. Re-sources are used to grow, manufacture, package and transport the item. And you only need to take a look at the statistics to realize that our current rate of con-sumerism is not sustainable. Did you know that every day, Americans throw out enough to fill 63,000 garbage trucks?[6] If the entire world wanted to live like this, we would need two more Earths. Last time we checked, we don't have a plan B planet! Although Elon Musk world argue that creating life on Mars is the solution to the damage we are inflicting on our planet.[7]

So what's the antidote? Simply put, minimalism. Minimalists buy quality over quantity and consider several factors before purchasing anything:

- Why do I need it?
- Is it something that I love and will use on a regular basis?
- How has it been made?
- Will it last, or will I need to buy a new one next year?
- Does it address a real need in my life (as opposed to an imaginary one)?
- Do I already own something similar?

Don't get us wrong; it takes work, hard work, to un-train your brain and free yourself from the passion you may feel for shopping. Most people become consumers because it feels good. It feels good for that split second, an hour, or a day. We go home so excited and happy with the item, share it with our loved ones, and the following month it's already been pushed to the back of the cupboard and forgotten about.

How do we move away from this constant buying mentality? By only purchasing things that add value to you. When you do, you're more likely to keep it for a long time and look after it. Instead of heading to the cheap fast fashion stores and going for the latest trends, designed to be worn once and tossed aside for the next style. Buy yourself a timeless piece instead. Even if it's more expensive, buy a beautiful outfit that can be worn for many occasions, fits perfectly and is made to last. This would be a much wiser investment.

Did you know that over 13 million tons of textiles are trashed every year, in the US alone?[8],[9] Imagine what that would look like on a global scale. Only 15% of this is recovered for recycling.[10] And with fast throw-away fashion labeled the second most polluting industry globally, you've got another great reason to streamline your wardrobe.[11]

Decluttering your mind as well as your physical and digital possessions will free you up for the more essential things in life, and you can entirely dictate those things. There's beauty in simple living.

Consumerism is like an endless black hole: you end up wasting so much time and energy desiring, obtaining and then dealing with a mountain of things, and trying to claw back a little bit of your mental and physical space. There's nothing wrong with empty corners and clear minds. No wonder meditation and yoga practices have exploded into the mainstream over the last couple of decades. People want to feel connected to themselves, their lives and their environment, become more mindful and in turn live more consciously.

It's time to put modern society's consumerist drive to one side and move into minimalism.

TRAPPED IN YOUR OWN STUFF

It's pretty logical. The more stuff you own, the more managing you have to do. The amount of energy, and time can be overwhelming and you may feel like it's controlling you. If you're anything like us and you like tidy spaces, then you'll appreciate having less stuff around. Visual clutter can be the difference between a focused, clear mind or a confused cluttered mental space.

Day after day, we bring things into our homes. And we usually bring in much more than we take out.

29

This is where things become problematic. As each cupboard and surface gets taken over by things, so do our minds. Cleaning, tidying, organizing and finding things can take up a lot of our time. Why do we have such trouble getting rid of things? There are so many reasons we hold onto items we don't need. Let's explore some of them.

Keeping Things Out Of Guilt

We've all been there. A close relative lovingly gives us a mug. We look at it wondering why on earth we would want an old mug from the '60's? Besides, it doesn't match the style of the house, and we'd rather not have it sitting next to our glassware. But we feel like we need to keep it; we wouldn't want to hurt our relative's feelings. We feel guilty even thinking about giving it to charity or a friend that loves collectibles.

The conversation becomes easier with family and friends when they know you're a minimalist and you don't want physical things. This can take time though.

Our family and friends know that if they're going to gift us something, we'd prefer for it to be an experience. We have had some great memorable moments built around gifts like this.

Being Afraid To Let Go

The hardest kind will always be the sentimental items, especially items linked to important people who have passed. But people are not their things, and letting go of their possessions will not take away the memories. These memories are within us, and nothing can replace that. If you want to keep the memory of an item, take a photo of it. You don't need to physically keep it. If you strongly feel compelled to keep something, add it to your 'sentimental' box.

We each created a sentimental box. Whatever can fit in there and that really makes us happy, we keep. Remember though that we come into this world with no possessions, and we leave it the same way. Letting go of these attachments can be liberating.

It Was Free

A common reason our homes are filled with mountains of stuff is that we received them for free. In fact, one of the most influential words in advertising is "free."[12] Getting something for free makes us feel good for a host of reasons, from feeling cared for to feeling like we got a bargain. It triggers emotional responses too, like the fear of missing out. That's why even the thriftiest shopper will succumb to the temptation of something free. But in some situations, and indeed, in the long term, this addiction to free stuff doesn't do us much good. For instance, your sister has a big clear out and invites you over to see if you want anything before her garage sale or donation to charity. You have a poke around and see a super cute teapot. You fall in love with it and decide to take it with you. You do have the fleeting thought that you don't really need it since you already have one but you just can't bear the thought of someone else snatching it up. So now you have two teapots in the cupboard. You still use yours because it pours better and holds more tea. The other one just sits there, taking up space, until you move house or have a clear out of your own, and then it ends up in the donation box. You see how the lifecycle of that teapot could have been in the hands of another person that would have utilised it much sooner, and in turn leave you with more time and fewer decisions to make?

Multiply this scenario by ten. In our day-to-day lives, we have moments like this all the time, with there being a sale on every other day, and the people around us having regular clear outs to make more room for new sale items. But these things don't add value; they take it away. Instead of consuming your mind with additional buying choices, you can enjoy the benefits of having to make fewer decisions.

You Might Need It "One Day"

Another common scenario. The average shed is a perfect example, containing enough tools to build a small town. You buy heavy-duty equipment for that DIY project you've been promising to start since last spring or to fix that one door. Then it sits in the shed for ten years getting rusty.

When it comes to bulky gardening or DIY equipment, get creative. Could you make it work without actually owning the tool? Could you share the cost with family or friends? Or could you merely hire it, or even borrow your neighbor's?

Society as a whole has moved away from working as a community and borrowing things from a neighbor, friend or family member. When was the last time someone knocked on your door asking to borrow a hammer?

So It Doesn't "Go To Waste"

This one is for the thrifty among us. Those who want to save anything that might be of use. Because it is such a shame to throw it out, right? Like those neat little plastic packets of buttons and string that come with some new clothes. We add them to the pile we've been saving for fifteen years. Out of sight, out of mind? Not quite. Unfortunately, what you're left with are cluttered drawers and a cluttered brain.

Multi-Purpose Items

Reducing your possessions will create more mental and physical freedom. Take it to the next level. Get creative with your family to find ways of buying less by choosing items with multi-purpose uses, or that can be shared. Sharing is caring after all.

For example, rather than having men's, women's and kids shampoos, buy one that suits all hair types. Our hair is not all that different. Have one tablet between you instead of one for each person. Just take turns in using it. Have one car. We have had one car between us for the past three years. We work with each other and catch the bus or a ride where possible. Granted, we don't have a family, but we still decided to go with one car even though we have the means to use two. You'll be amazed at how many things (expensive ones at that) can be down sized and maximized with just a little bit of effort.

There are plenty of projects and ideas online that can help you move things out of your home. Simple strategies such as removing one item a day can feel liberating. After doing that for thirty, sixty, ninety days, your home will be transformed. And the good thing is that removing one item a day isn't overwhelming! The key here is just to get started and to discontinue bringing more in.

A Preventative Approach

True minimalism isn't about continually managing and eliminating things. This is more the stage before minimalism when you evaluate your possessions and see which ones you can scale down. Minimalism is more about mindfulness. When you're mindful in the first place, you make conscious choices about what you bring into your world. Like a preventative approach that allows you the mental and physical space to do what's important to you, and what brings you happiness.

DEVELOPING MINDFULNESS

Becoming a minimalist requires a touch of mindfulness. When you're mindful, you do things with intent. You create more space for important things in your life, like the people you love spending time with, and activities that stimulate you physically and emotionally. Here are some of the things that helped us develop mindfulness in our day-to-day lives.

Flip The Conversation In Your Mind

When we first think about minimalism, we often associate it with the elimination of things. While this is consistent with our philosophy, we've found that focusing more on what you want is more powerful than focusing on the things you want to let go of.

You hear it all the time with minimalism; "By eliminating X, it opened up my capacity for Y."

So why not reverse this approach and focus on what we want if we had the capacity? For example, let's say you wanted to get into shape but you're struggling because you're bogged down with too many commitments. Unless you have an extreme desire to get into shape (focusing on what you want) it's unlikely that you will have the consistent motivation to say no to some of the less critical tasks in your life (focusing on what you don't need).

So when we focus more on identifying what is important to us, maybe then we can start taking action towards cutting back on the things that hold us back.

Be Grateful For The Little Things

"The More Virus" is the enemy of contentment. Once you have assuaged one particular desire, it's on to the next one, because the item/job/weight loss never delivers long-term happiness. So you just keep wanting more more more.

When you think small and celebrate small, you free yourself from those unending desires. You are living every day with the things you have, and that's enough. Feel gratitude for the simple things, like having a roof over your head or being able to make a home-cooked meal, or spending an afternoon in nature with your family. Celebrating small and being grateful makes you happier... no purchase is necessary.

Find Happiness In The Present

How many times have you thought along the lines of: "When I find my dream partner, then I will be happy." You may be wondering what this has to do with minimalism. A lot. If we are continually placing our happiness in the future and making it dependent on external factors, we'll be forever seeking it and only ever fleetingly be finding it. To practice and understand minimalism and gratitude, we need to feel happy and content with what we have right now. Not when we win the lottery or when the weekend comes around or when we get married.

Many of us are so focused on the future that we are never genuinely present or enjoy the moment that is now. We put our happiness on hold because we don't have certain things. But when you think about it, the present moment is all we have. After all, yesterday is gone and cannot be changed. And tomorrow is a construct of the mind. It doesn't exist. When tomorrow comes, it is today.

If we keep dreaming and waiting for tomorrow, we are missing out on the beauty that is around us right now. Take a step back and enjoy the reality that you have in this very moment, in this breath. No one knows what tomorrow may bring, why not make the most of today?

Don't Be Afraid To Miss Out

Ah, good old FOMO (fear of missing out). You're not alone in feeling it. How many of us keep our Facebook accounts for fear that if we close it, we'll ultimately lose touch with all our friends and never be invited to the fantastic events? How many of us compulsively watch the news or check news websites for the latest on world events in fear of looking stupid if we don't know "all the facts?"

Why are you afraid of "missing out?" Is it the fear that others will judge you? Or the worry that you won't find that perfect pair of bargain designer shoes? Or anxiety over not being "in the know?" FOMO is one way advertisers grab our attention. "This amazing deal won't last" but two weeks later there's another mid-season sale with half-price discounts on overpriced furniture. Fear of missing out is just another way of being disconnected from the present moment. And living in fear is no way to live. So, shift your focus of missing out into an opportunity to recognize what you are afraid of and do something that makes you happy instead. Turn your fear of missing out into the joy of missing out (JOMO).

Celebrating and being grateful for the simple things in your life is an amazing way to start shifting your mindset to a minimalist lifestyle. Creating intent around everything that you do and buy will, in turn, help you focus on the essential things, and live with more meaning.

Being content can sometimes feel like a tricky thing to achieve, especially in our retail-driven world. But it just takes a little practice and dedication. Every time you notice that you are focusing on fear (of missing out, not reaching your goal, or not finding the perfect pair of shoes), choose instead to be grateful and to return to the present moment with love.

COURAGEOUSLY SIMPLE

Achieving simplicity in life is hard. It takes time and effort to break old habits, simplify your lifestyle and start doing things that matter. With so many things competing for our attention, we can quickly go through each day getting through tasks and chores without any passion or thought. Lost in the whirlwind of busyness, forever chasing the next to-do, it's no wonder we feel that we don't have the time to stop and rethink our current way of life. As one day turns into a week, a month, a year, a decade, we have a choice: keep going full steam ahead on autopilot, or have the courage to press the pause button, step out of our comfort zone, begin ruthlessly simplifying, and uncover magic.

We need to dare ourselves to be different. To separate ourselves from what society deems "normal." And normal these days means working three jobs or climbing the corporate ladder, endless consuming, rushing from place to place and person to person. We wear busyness as a badge of honor, as part of a "work hard, play hard" mentality, but most of us are too busy ever to play. And the sad thing is that, while being busy is seen as a positive, if you're forever busy chances are you're not taking enough time out for yourself, for your loved ones, or to do the things that make you truly happy. It's time to stop feeling like we need to blend in with the crowd and continue the ever-quickening rat race. Of course, this requires some commitment and outside the box thinking. And it begins with the decision to say no to the things that don't honestly matter.

But most of us are dreadfully uncomfortable with that concept. Why is it so hard to break away from it?

As humans, we seek comfort in having more. More acts as a security blanket. An example of that security blanket is:

- Having the compulsion to pack two suitcases for a week's holiday (just in case I need it).

- Buying more food (usually because of special offers, discounts or the sake of "topping up").

- Saying yes to social engagements we don't feel like going to (for fear of missing out or letting people down).

Being busy is another security blanket we use to comfort ourselves into feeling that our lives are complete and meaningful. This security blanket mentality keeps us from simplifying.

Simplifying your life isn't as "simple" as the word implies, namely because it takes a lot of courage to go against the grain, to decide to cut out the superfluous in your life and focus on things that make you happy.

But once you've made that decision, take that first step; you'll be amazed how easy it becomes.

So how can we make life simpler and live like a minimalist? Well, the first step is to dive into the very core of things, what matters. For example, you're working two jobs to make ends meet but as a consequence, you hardly ever get time to spend an evening cozied up on the sofa with your partner, so your relationship may be suffering. You don't enjoy your work and wish you could do something different, like travel for a year, set up your own business, learn to sculpt, or maybe you just want more time to yourself or for your family, but you're afraid of what people might think. So you follow the same routine day in day out. Running from tedious job, to chores, spending every moment wishing you could do what you loved but never having the time or the courage to begin throwing away the shackles, sweeping away the unnecessary, and designing a life tailored to what you want to experience. But imagine if you could clear your schedule of additional commitments, and spend a little time first to understand what matters to you, prioritize what you're passionate about, and then to begin taking the steps towards the life you want. That's what we mean by simplifying life. Not a life of white wall minimalism and 24/7 in solitary meditation. A life decluttered of superfluous things, leaving you with time to focus on what makes you happy.

Of course, simplifying your life requires courage, as you'll first have to be brave enough to look at the areas of your life that need to be clarified, and secondly, you'll have to learn to say no. No to events and people that don't honestly bring you joy. No to weekly commitments that fill up your time and take you away from focusing on what matters to you. No to your inner voice who wants the comfort of the familiar and might be telling you to delay diving into minimalism because you just don't have the time.

Think about your life and how you want it to look. Consider how much time you want to spend doing the things you love, spending time with the people you love, doing charity work or simply taking time for self-care. Looking at your weekly schedule and writing down what is important to you will help guide your decisions. At each conclusion, ask yourself: "Will this contribute to my happiness? Will it add simplicity to my life or take it away?" You'll soon develop a mindset that will make decision-making much more natural and instinctive. Just like minimalism, there's no one-size-fits-all model for simplifying life—it all very much depends on how you want your life to look, what brings you happiness, what you are passionate about, what matters to you. By beginning to peel away what isn't essential, you can reveal the beautiful simplicity of life beyond the trappings of "The More Virus" and the modern rat-race.

Simplicity is beautiful and at times elusive, but it's also worth fighting for. You need to be courageous to do it, but when you do, the rewards are priceless.

MISCONCEPTIONS OF MINIMALISM

There are so many myths and misconceptions about minimalism. We personally used to think that it was boring, white walls, white furniture (not much at that), and no style. A lot of people think this way. But actually, there are no hard and fast rules, no handbook decreeing that you must own fewer than three pairs of pants and only one set of cutlery. Minimalism can be adapted to your lifestyle.

The essence of minimalism is to keep only what is essential and what truly brings joy to you, and eliminate the rest.

So, we want to share and debunk some of the minimalist myths we have come across.

You Can Only Own a Limited Number of Items

Minimalism is a way of life, not about counting how many belongings you own. Sure, some people thrive on that kind of approach and pride themselves on only possessing one hundred items or less. But there's no right or wrong way. If the things are being used or serve an important purpose, keep them.

You Have To Throw Everything Away

We had a freak-out moment when we first thought about this concept. Maša's reaction was a very definite "Don't take away all my pretty things!" But once you start to understand what it means and why you are doing it, many of those 'pretty things' stop having much meaning. And you'll discover which ones add value.

You also don't have to throw everything away. Just go through all your belongings and make a conscious choice: keep or remove? No more boxes of old paperwork. No more bags of unwanted clothes. Feel the sense of freedom that comes from a home filled only with items you truly want there.

No More Shopping Ever Again

Minimalists don't just buy everyday essentials like food and toilet paper. Now and then minimalists need new sneakers or a blender. The difference is that everything is bought with intention. Not because it's on sale or because it soothes a materialistic desire.

There's a vast difference between consuming aimlessly and buying with intent.

Minimalism Makes You Boring

We thought minimalism was boring before we truly understood the concept. We thought minimalists didn't appreciate or have art in their homes, enjoy stylish furniture or fashion, and were pretty bland people in general.

We can tell you now, having shifted our lifestyle, that you can be a vibrant, stylish, fashionable minimalist. It's all about quality, not quantity. You can pick out an amazing outfit that will last you at least ten years because it's made from quality, organic and fair trade materials and looks stunning on you. We still enjoy all the things we did before becoming minimalists. We just choose wisely, keeping the environment and animals in mind.

Minimalism Is Bad For Business

Some might argue a minimalist society would be detrimental to commerce. We believe the opposite. If every person lived with such awareness, unethical businesses would be exposed, and successful companies would be the ones creating ethical, green solutions that last longer, perform better and protect our planet. We love imagining a world where everyone is a minimalist. What would that look like? Primarily, it would reverse the consumerist mindset that's embedded so deeply in the way most of us live today.

We hope that mindfulness will be the key motivator for both consumers and business moving forward. And it starts with all of us rethinking how we want to consume.

The Power of Minimalism

You see, minimalism doesn't need to be scary or complicated.

Instead of accumulating things, wouldn't it be more beautiful to spend your hard earned money on experiences? We have learned to value experiences over possessions. Experiences are what create a memorable life: the thrill of exploring somewhere new, the feelings born of doing something different, the excitement of trying a new hobby, the people you share this with. We can assure you that no one on their deathbed wishes they spent more money on things. They wish they'd taken that leap of faith, spent more time with people they care about or explored more of the world. Remember, we come into this world with nothing, and we leave it with nothing. Fill your life with emotion, excitement, memories, and love. These are the things that will leave a lasting impression on you and everyone that you cross paths with.

More things do not equate to more happiness. Becoming a minimalist will help you detach from the illusion that shopping brings you joy. When you adopt a minimalist mindset, you become more mindful of how your choices affect you and the world, and you can, therefore, shift your habits to support your happiness and global sustainability.

Are you ready to take that mindset to the next level, into veganism?

LEAD WITH COMPASSION

We'd like to begin this chapter with how we define veganism because everyone sees it slightly differently. For us, it means choosing a lifestyle that does the least harm to animals, our planet, and our health. It goes beyond merely avoiding animal products, and deeper into where the product came from, how it was made, and who produced it. Veganism is a lifestyle choice with roots set firmly in compassion.

We need to change how we view animals. When you look at the world, we are treating each other, nature and all other living beings with disrespect. We need to start treating everything with the same amount of compassion as we treat ourselves.

Compassion For Animals And The Planet

The word compassion is an interesting one. The literal meaning is: "Sympathetic pity and concern for the sufferings or misfortunes of others."[13] The suffering of others is what we want to highlight. Most people don't want another living being to suffer. We might think we sometimes do, like the fleeting thoughts that accompany a heated argument, but deep down no one, at least so we hope, wants to inflict suffering on another. Those of us who have pets know that they could never support the torture or murder of their beloved furry friends, but how is a cow, hen or lamb any different from a cat or dog in that respect? Do we align with the notion that we can determine a sentient being's right to live based on how they look? Speciesism is as unacceptable as sexism and racism. If you feel compassion towards a domesticated animal, why not others?

These animals didn't choose to end up in a feedlot. This destiny was handed to them. Billions of animals each year end up the same way. Treated appallingly for the short time it takes the artificial feed to fatten them up enough to make them fit for slaughter, just for our selfish desires. Now, we use the word selfish because, with so many vegan alternatives nowadays, at least in the Western world, we don't need to eat the flesh and secretions of other beings to stay healthy. It goes back to a powerful quote from Pam Ahern, "If we could live happy and healthy lives without harming others, why wouldn't we?" Most of us choose meat for the taste, convenience and the fact that we've always done it. Think about it, would we eat as much meat if we had to kill a pig every time we wanted a bacon sandwich, or strangle a hen every time we wanted chicken nuggets to snack on? We don't think so somehow.

And yet when we buy meat, dairy, or other animal-derived products, we are supporting an industry that consciously mistreats animals. Study after study has shown that animals feel pain, sorrow, suffering, love, and loss.[14] Rather than try to manage animal farming humanely, the most prominent meat producers spend much of their time coming up with ways of cutting costs to maximize profits. This means smaller pens, dangerous working conditions, growth hormones, antibiotics, bigger machines, faster conveyor belts. It's an industry that treats its employees like dirt, the planet as its toilet, and animals as commodities. An industry that produces food (if you want to call it food) that, despite being artificially cheap (usually thanks to government subsidies), has a substantial environmental, social and health cost.[15] An industry that doesn't even know the meaning of compassion.

If you think however that grass-fed is more sustainable, even though it may be slightly more humane to the animals, it's an environmental disaster. Grass-fed cattle are no doubt happier than their feed-lot counterparts: they have more room to move, eat a natural diet, and don't get pumped full of antibiotics and artificial feed. As a result, they are healthier, stronger animals. However, raising grass-fed livestock for slaughter takes around eight months longer.[16] That's eight months worth of food, water, excrement, methane... not to mention how much more land is needed for pasture compared to land required for intensive animal farming. If we wanted to switch all livestock to grass-fed, most of the world would turn into grazing land. It's just not sustainable.[17] We're not advocating animal farming one bit, just pointing out that while grass-fed organic beef may better for your health then factory-farmed, it's definitely not better for the planet and cannot be considered sustainable. Either way, you look at it, whether the animal is raised "humanely" or not, when their time is up, they are sent to slaughter. The outcome is the same. So raising them in different ways still gives them the inevitable future of ending up on your dinner table. There's no real "humane" way to kill and eat animals, period.

Somewhere along the line, humans decided that they were superior to animals. Yes, at some point in our history, one might argue that a human's ability to survive was dependent on the death of animals. However, fast forward to today, with the overconsumption of animal products and the rise of plant-based alternatives, the practice of exploiting animals is unnecessary. On the other hand, we need animals to survive. Without bees, for example, we would lose a third of our plant foods.[18] Without insects, the soil becomes barren. And without the modern trappings of tools and weapons, we do not stand a chance against the world's natural predators.

Some people think that nature needs humans to manage it. But nature was beautiful before humans began trying to control it with synthetic fertilizers, genetic engineering, and fossil fuel extraction. If humans disappeared from the planet, nature would thrive, rebalance and heal.[19] So why not start making a change today and start working with nature instead of against it? Through veganism—compassion for animals, people, and our planet—we can begin reversing the damage we've inflicted on the Mother Nature.

Let's take a look at how the meat industry impacts our planet, beyond the atrocities it commits on animals.

Environment

Since documentaries like Cowspiracy hit the mainstream screens, it has become impossible to avoid the devastating environmental consequences of industrial meat production. Even with the spread of undeniable evidence, as reported by internationally recognized organizations like the United Nations' Food and Agriculture Organization (FAO), the United States Environmental Protection Agency (EPA), the Environmental Working Group (EWG), the World Wildlife Fund (WWF), the Center for Biological Diversity, and countless others, many still believe that diet and the environment are two unrelated topics.[20] They are absolutely linked. More than linked: intensive animal farming happens to be one of the leading causes of global warming.[21] Big statement to make, we know, and one that makes many people uncomfortable, but the data speaks for itself. Animal agriculture and fishing are to blame for species extinction, ocean dead zones, land desertification, water pollution and habitat destruction.[22] Understanding how devastating your dietary choices can be will help you to make healthier and more sustainable choices.

Water

Water is precious. While it is essential to all life, clean water is a scarce commodity. All over the world, conflicts are erupting to gain control over this vital resource.[23],[24] So how does it make sense, when millions of people around the globe do not have enough fresh water to drink, to pump 50 trillion gallons a year (and that's in the United States alone) into producing meat?[25]

By the way, that's more than the water wasted on fracking (between 70 and 140 billion gallons, in case you're wondering).[26] And that makes animal agriculture worse than one of the most polluting and wasteful modern practices.

50 trillion gallons. It's a mind-blowing number, but when you consider how many animals this involves, it all makes sense. Well, how about this for perspective: to produce just one pound of beef takes 2,500 gallons of water. That's enough water for 17.2 years of healthy hydration, based on drinking the recommended 0.3 gallon/1.5 liters of water a day.[27]

So, just to recap. On the one hand you have a pound of beef (enough to feed four people once, as long as you've got veggies and a dessert to accompany it), and on the other hand, you've got enough water to keep four people hydrated for over four years. Or, as one of the Cowspiracy directors put it, just one hamburger patty is equivalent to two months' worth of showers. Something's not right!

The eco-friendly water-saving measures you might take, like quicker showers, turning off the tap when you brush your teeth, shorter wash cycles, all pale into insignificance when you consider how much water you save by merely choosing to go meatless.

And let's not forget our oceans. Fishing nets do not discriminate. For every pound of edible fish, they catch five pounds of "collateral," or "by-kill" as it's known in the trade: species that are of little use to food manufacturers, and that are tossed overboard. Sharks, dolphins, whales, turtles, all the rich diversity of our seas are quickly being dredged up and killed. For nothing. At this rate, our oceans will be empty by 2048.[28] And that doesn't just mean empty of fish; it means completely dead: too toxic for life to thrive. Australia's Great Barrier Reef is a sobering example of what is happening because of global warming, pollution, and intensive farming: two-thirds are dead or dying.[29] In just 30 years, our oceans will become barren deserts, and the only things floating there will be the trillions of plastic bottles we've thrown in. Isn't the genuine danger of the earth's most precious ecosystem becoming an empty wasteland enough of a reason to change our lifestyles and our diets? It doesn't seem like much of a 'sacrifice' if you ask us.

Land

One of our jaw-drop moments came when we discovered how much of the world's land is used for livestock: over 45% in 2011.[30] That's nearly half the land on this planet! All of this for animals who are then mistreated, overfed, then killed. Ending up on our dinner table, or handed to us in a paper bag, stuffed between two soggy halves of a plastic bun.

Every second, two acres of land is cleared to make space for livestock or to grow grain to feed them. In just the time it took you to read this sentence, another five acres have been grazed down.[31] All over the world, ancient rainforests, home to thousands of rare and precious species, are mindlessly cut down, burnt down, and swept away to make room for cattle or crops.[32] Every day, around 130 animal, plant and insect species become extinct as a direct result of animal agriculture.[33] Creatures that have evolved over millennia are simply wiped out because of our culture's love of cheap, abundant meat.

Pollution

Cows are big animals. And they produce a lot of excrement. Just in the United States, 7 million pounds of excrement are created every minute.[34] Every minute. Now, aside from the appalling stench and serious yuk factor, it's a huge environmental problem as this mountain of toxic poop has to go somewhere. That somewhere happens to be the environment at large. It leaches into the soil, contaminates fresh water sources, and ends up in our oceans.[35],[36] Some industrial farms are inventive and spray the muck into the air as a means to deal with it, making the lives of anyone unfortunate enough to live nearby an absolute stinking misery. Antibiotics from cow poop have been found in drinking water in quite a few major American regions as well.[37] Pretty scary stuff.

Putting poop to one side but staying in that department for a second, cows fart. And those farts are lethal because they are methane farts. As far as global warming goes, methane is 25-100 times more destructive than CO_2![38] Essentially, what is coming out of livestock bottoms is more dangerous for our planet than what is coming out of our car exhausts!

But of course, that doesn't mean cattle aren't also responsible for plenty of CO_2. In fact, as early as 2009 alarm bells started ringing when a study reported that livestock and their by-products were responsible for over 32,000 million tons of carbon dioxide a year, which equated to 51% of worldwide greenhouse gas emissions.[39],[40]

Worse still, intensive animal farming practices speed up global warming. How? Remember deforestation? Livestock is responsible for up to 91% of rainforest destruction.[41] Beyond the habitat destruction and species decimation, deforestation removes the planet's filtering system. Rainforests aren't called the planet's lungs for nothing. Trees absorb CO_2, that's one of the many reasons we need to protect them, es-

pecially today. Without them, the planet slowly suffo-
cates, meaning we slowly suffocate.

This is why we need to send a message, loud and
clear, by choosing to leave the steak on the shelf. There
is power in numbers, and if we stop buying it, there
will be less and less demand for it.

Society And Justice

Veganism goes beyond animal torture, mistreatment
and consumption. It looks at the entire supply chain.
The meat industry is one of the most dangerous sec-
tors to work in.[42] The injury rate in meat packing
plants is three times higher than other factories.[43] It is
hard to imagine that anyone would choose to work in a
factory slitting an animal's throat every five seconds for
ten hours a day, or wading through ankle-deep blood,
dodging and hacking away at carcasses. But these
workers are often migrants, unprotected by unions,
forced to work long hours in hellish environments for
barely enough to survive.[44] All this because of western
culture's obsession with cheap meat.

News websites or channels fail to give sufficient attention to the devastating effects of animal agriculture because it requires a fundamental change in behavior. The focus is on other planet-saving tips like taking shorter showers, cycling or catching public transport, recycling and using your own shopping bags. None of this gets close to the impact of going meatless. But, if you're truly serious about creating a sustainable world, reducing meat and dairy consumption will have the greatest impact.

When we look at that neatly packaged chicken breast or rashers of bacon, it's easy not to see the death, destruction and suffering it implies. But what lurks behind the sanitized cellophane is environmental decimation, worker exploitation, and social injustice. Isn't it time we stopped supporting this industry?

THE SUPERIOR SPECIES

Speciesism by definition means: "The assumption of human superiority leading to the exploitation of animals."[45] Why do we believe that we are superior to other species? Aren't we all animals? What separates us from other species? Consciousness? Communication? The ability to think? The ability to feel pain, loss, happiness, love? But animals feel things too—they feel emotions, pain, loss, affection.[46],[47] They seek companionship, they communicate, they are conscious of their environment. In some ways, they are superior to us.

They hear sounds our ears will never pick up, see things our eyes are incapable of, their sense of smell is more developed than ours could ever be, and even the most sophisticated fighter jet is cumbersome and clunky compared to the swift, graceful flight of a swallow. We may not entirely be able to understand their thinking, behavior, or the way they speak to each other. But that doesn't take away from the fact that, in every way that matters, all species are the same: we live on planet earth, we breathe the same air, we feel, we need food, water, shelter, and love, and we're here for a limited time. Surely, all species should have the right to a decent life? Claiming to be better than certain species, agreeing to the exploitation of other species, is puzzling. Does speciesism have space in a humane world?

As humans, we assume that we are superior to animals. We assume this because they have no voice. And we assume this because it suits us. They don't have a voice to protest when a cow's babies are ripped from her at birth so that humans can drink her milk. They don't have a voice when pigs are locked up in cages so small that they start biting each other's tails because they are either hungry or frustrated.[48] They don't have a voice to decry the throwing of baby male chicks into a grinder while they are still alive.[49] They don't have a voice to denounce the hunting of endangered species for their tusks, furs, and fins. These animals are seen as mere commodities. Not feeling, thinking, living beings, but indefensible objects to be exploited and abused for human sport, food, clothes, and entertainment.

Most of us turn away from these uncomfortable truths, but by doing so, we are complicit. By refusing to see the exploitation, torture, and murder of animals, and continuing to buy these products, we are effectively saying it's okay. And it is far from okay. Why do we believe we're superior to others? The way humans behave says: we are in favor of one species, ours, over all others. Are we the highest kind of animal because we exploit the billions that don't fall under the human privilege? Is that really what we, as humans, want to be? Are we a species of exploiters? A species who is slowly but surely destroying all other species on the planet to serve our needs?

Let's take it back to a few human examples. What about slavery, racism, and sexism? Unacceptable, right? Yet these are all forms of the same superiority complex: the belief that someone is better than another, and has rights over another, based on them being different. Today, we have a completely different view on slavery to what we had only two hundred years ago. Yes, slavery still exists in certain parts of the world today, such as child labor and human trafficking, and sweat-shop workers, to name but a few, however, it is not acceptable out in the open. If you knew that a child was taken from his or her parents and forced to pick cacao beans to make that cheap chocolate bar, you most likely wouldn't support it by buying it. This is why we are seeing more companies introducing fair-trade practices, to help consumers support brands that are doing the right thing. But what about the animals? What about being transparent about how the milk that's in your chocolate bar was obtained? Shouldn't that also be a fair-trade issue? If an animal has been exploited, mistreated, abused to make a product or for your entertainment, don't you want to know about it so that you can choose not to contribute to this industry? If humans weren't paid for their work and were kept in the same conditions animals endure, it would be all over the news. However, every single year, billions of animals suffer and work for us without being paid even in decent living conditions, and we still choose to support it blindly.

Entertainment

What is the first image that comes to mind when you think of slavery? For us, it's a person (typically a black person) with a chain around their neck marking them as property, who needs to obey their "owner." Arguably, this is what is done to animals today. And we don't even mean animals used in the meat, leather, dairy and egg industries. There's also all the animals in circuses, racing, zoos and entertainment parks. We have monetized animals against their will and their natural state of being. Horses have no innate desire to race against each other at the mercy of their jockey's whip, and orcas don't want to jump through hoops in tiny tanks for crowds of spectators. It's a myth to believe animals are taught tricks with love and the promise of treats, and certainly, this is a more convenient truth. But the fact is wild animals have to be forced to behave in ways that are not instinctive: trainers have to use violence to assert a position of dominance and keep the animals in check.[50]

Thanks to animal activists, big businesses like the Ringling Bros Circus have been left with no choice but to phase out all their animal acts. SeaWorld has been under scrutiny all around the globe for their treatment of whales, orcas, and dolphins. Their profits are plummeting at a rapid rate thanks to documentaries like Blackfish raising awareness of the truth behind these animal performance shows. [51] People are speaking up and refusing to support it. Times are changing, but not fast enough.

The opinion that animals don't feel emotion and pain like humans do is outdated. Countless studies now prove that animals do feel; in fact, they have a full range of emotions, including love, joy, happiness, shame, embarrassment, fear, resentment, jealousy, rage, compassion, respect, relief, disgust, sadness, despair and grief.[52] Even Charles Darwin, whose theory of evolution is sometimes used as an argument for the exploitation of animals, argues in his book *The Expression of the Emotions in Man and Animals*, that there are similarities between how humans and animals feel emotions. "Animals," he claims, "manifestly feel pleasure and pain, happiness, and misery." In other words, humans do not hold the monopoly on feeling and emotions. Some might argue that because animals' brains are not as large, or constructed in the same way as a human brain, animals are physically unable to feel. Again, this is inaccurate. The Cambridge Declaration of Consciousness, written by a prominent group of cognitive neuroscientists, neuropharmacologists, neurophysiologists, neuroanatomists and computational neuroscientists, states: "The absence of a neocortex does not appear to preclude an organism from experiencing affective states. Convergent evidence indicates that non-human animals have the neuroanatomical, neurochemical, and neurophysiological substrates of conscious states along with the capacity to exhibit intentional behaviors.[53] Consequently, the weight of evidence indicates that humans are not unique in possessing the neurological substrates that generate consciousness. Non-human animals, including all mammals and birds, and many other creatures, including octopuses, also possess these neurological substrates."[54]

This becomes obvious any time you see or hear an animal behave, the noises they make when they are excited or in fear. They communicate in the same way as a baby might, or even an adult with learning disabilities. But we don't punish babies or people with a disability or think any less of them, purely based on the fact that they are the same species as us. We need to extend that respect to non-human species too.

Just because they look different, communicate differently, behave differently, does not give us the right to treat other living creatures with cruelty or apathy. Given the evidence that animals experience the same emotions we do, why don't we put ourselves in their shoes, and imagine what it might be like to live in captivity, in cramped, squalid conditions, with little food, forced to perform at will or aware of the cruel fate that awaits? If we put ourselves in their shoes, it would become impossible to justify the pain and suffering we inflict on animals in the name of fashion, entertainment, food... and even science.

Animal Testing

In the name of science: this is one side of animal cruelty that we find tends to be justified the most (besides the alleged health benefits of eating animals and their by-products). Many rats, mice, rabbits, cats, dogs, primates and guinea pigs are bred specifically for animal testing.[55] Where do you think the saying "I'm happy to be your guinea pig" came from? You probably wouldn't be so willing to be anyone's guinea pig when you consider that research animals are electroshocked, pumped full of toxic chemicals, mutilated in experimental surgeries, given cancerous tumors, drilled alive, force-fed, burnt, kept in overcrowded cages and disposed of like rubbish.[56]

Here again, animals are treated as mere objects that we can use for research purposes in science and product testing. Some of the world's best-known makeup brands, like Estée Lauder, Clinique, Maybelline, Clarins, Origins and Bobbi Brown, to name but a few, pay for animal testing to be carried out in China.[57] But it isn't just makeup. Household items like bleach, dishwashing liquid, and air freshener are tested on animals. Tests involve giving the animals high doses of toxic chemicals or rubbing irritants into their eyes and skin. Even diapers are tested: animals are forced to eat the ingredients used in diapers to detect allergic reactions.[58] If you want to make sure you're only buying brands that don't test on animals, some great apps can help, like Cruelty-Free and Choose Cruelty-Free.[59],[60]

Some researchers argue that animal testing is essential for "fundamental research" (research that may be used medically in the future), but according to Cruelty-Free International, less than 5% of the discoveries made from animal experiments result in approved health treatments.[61]

Genetically modifying animals for research is an increasingly popular practice, which involves breeding animals with certain genes added or taken away. Many of these animals die very young as a result of these genetic manipulations. What's more, experiments using genetically modified animals are flawed as they cannot mimic the complexity of human diseases.[62] For instance, most cases of cancer and heart disease are caused by lifestyle factors rather than genetics.[63],[64]

Would we do the same form of testing on a human as we do on animals? Most people would answer no. The suffering caused to them is based on the concept that they are unfeeling beings, rooted in the fact they belong to a different species, and yet they feel the same type of pain as we would if we were lab rats.

Once we recognize that speciesism is a problem, it is no longer possible to support practices that use animals as mere objects, tools or playthings there for human entertainment and nothing more. We are not the superior species. We are one species among 8.7 million on earth, and now more than ever, we need to learn to respect them and share our planet with them.[65]

BEHIND THE FASHION LABEL

Veganism isn't just about what you put on your plate, but also what you choose to put on your body. Big food and fashion industries are similar concerning how they exploit animals, waste resources and pollute our planet. We need to extend our compassion to the choices we make about what we wear as much as what we eat.

High street fashion chains rely on a high volume of sales. These days, stores no longer have a spring/summer and fall/winter collection. Instead, they offer ceaselessly changing styles and products designed to be loved for a few weeks, before being tossed aside and replaced. But for this business model to be profitable, the items need to be cheap to make, so that they can be offered at a low price. Let's be honest, how likely would we be to buy a t-shirt every other week if that t-shirt cost $90 instead of $10—in other words if the cost of an item reflected the work and materials that went into it?

Fast fashion needs cheap costs to drive sales, so prices are cut at nearly every link in the chain: overseas labor, child labor, toxic materials produced in countries where there are no environmental or workers' rights regulations. Subcontractors (most often sub-sub-sub-contractors) are hired, which are impossible to monitor, allowing brands to pass the buck of social and environmental responsibility.[66]

The result is an industry that, regarding unethical practices, environmental consequences, animal cruelty and worker injustice, isn't far behind animal agriculture.

Dangerous Working Conditions

Not only are workers paid a pittance, they often have to deal with unsanitary and hazardous conditions.[67] An investigation by Human Rights Watch examined the leather industry in Bangladesh and found children working in tanneries without protective gear, exposed to acid, chemicals, and toxic fumes. They work ten hour days, earning less than $40 a month. And yet in the last decade, leather exports have grown by around $41 million each year.[68] The profits are certainly not going to the workers.

Animal Cruelty

Leather is obtained in many different ways, none of which are humane. Cheap leather is often sourced from India, China or Bangladesh, where cows, pigs, goats, cats, and dogs end up as inexpensive "100% genuine" leather goods.[69] A recent PETA investigation revealed how dogs are abused, tortured and killed in a

Chinese factory, and turned into cheap leather gloves, belts, and fur trims.[70]

Some people think leather is merely a by-product of the meat industry—a resource that would otherwise go to waste. We've all used this argument to make ourselves feel better about buying that leather bag. Unfortunately, leather is not a by-product of the animal industry, but a co-product without which the industry could not survive.[71] Most cow leather comes from cows that are no longer producing enough milk to be profitable. As for the more "luxurious" leather (thinner and softer, used for "premium" products), this comes from newborn calves, sometimes even unborn calves, snatched prematurely from their mother's womb. There's nothing ethical, fair or desirable about leather products.

But it isn't just leather. Many of the sheep sheared for their wool, including cashmere and angora goats, usually die from cold exposure. Shearing is done in a rush, with no thought to the sheeps' wellbeing, their wounds go untreated or sewn together with needle and thread. Before being slaughtered for their pelt, lambs suffer brutal procedures like castration without anesthetic. They live in cramped, squalid conditions, in fear and pain. Fur farms are notorious for using the most inhumane slaughter procedures like electrocution, suffocation, and poison. Some shearers skin the animals alive. Exotic wools, like Shahtoosh, and furs (like bear, seal, beaver, and others) come from wild animals that are trapped and killed for their skin.[72],[73]

Down is just as cruel as leather or fur. Birds are raised, again in sardine-tin like conditions, periodically strung up, their down ripped from them, their torn skin sewn up, and tossed aside until the next feather harvest. The birds that do not die during this process are eventually sold to the poultry industry, killed and turned into meat or foie gras.[74]

Whether fur farmed or wild caught, there's nothing ethical or desirable about wearing another being's skin, and the more we demand cheap leather jackets and ever-changing fashion, the more we are supporting an industry based on animal cruelty.

Environmental Impact

Fast fashion has a substantial environmental impact too. Did you know it takes nearly 4,400 gallons of water to produce just one pair of jeans?[75]

Most cotton crops are now grown with genetically modified cotton seeds from pharmaceutical giants like Monsanto. These crops, ironically enough, need to be sprayed with increasing amounts of glyphosate herbicides, which leach into the soil, contaminate groundwater, and end up in our rivers and oceans, decimating wildlife.[76]

It also takes a lot of chemical fertilizers to grow non-organic cotton—roughly a third of a pound for every pound of cotton (around the amount needed to make a t-shirt). These fertilizers pollute groundwater and emit nitrous oxide, a greenhouse gas 300 times more destructive than CO_2.[77]

Beyond the outer environment, these chemicals affect our inner world as well. Glyphosate has been classified by the International Agency for Research on Cancer as "probably carcinogenic to humans."[78] It's a known endocrine disrupter (it disrupts hormones), which causes a host of health complications from diabetes to thyroid disease.[79] These chemicals linger on fast fashion clothes and can be absorbed through the skin.[80] Their effects on animals are also well documented, with recent studies showing that glyphosate is genotoxic (negatively affects cells' DNA) and causes reproductive problems.[81]

Clearly, fast fashion and cheap clothing aren't compatible with a minimalist, vegan lifestyle. So what can we do?

Cruelty-Free Clothing

It's all about supply and demand. Fashion industries are only profitable because we buy their products. But when you buy fashion you're not just paying the designer; you're supporting the entire supply chain—that's why it's so important to vote with your dollar. Turn away from cheap fashion labels and instead buy from ethical, cruelty-free brands. There are plenty to choose from these days, with styles to satisfy the most fashion conscious among us.

NOWHERE TO GO

When we think of animal cruelty, most of us think of animals in the food or entertainment industry. Dogs and cats are our friends, and most of us treat our pets as part of the family. But where did our beloved pets come from? An online shop? A pet store perhaps? Or an animal shelter? Many of us don't hear or think about how our pets came into this world, or what kind of conditions parents and puppies live in until they land in our arms. If your dog comes from an online shop or pet store, chances are (in 99% of cases) that your puppy has come from a pet mill that treats animals not as living, conscious creatures, but as commodities.

Here is the typical story of how our puppies and kittens are brought into this world. Breeders often go to dog auctions to buy as many females and strong males for as little money as possible. It's said that the domestic pet industry is more lucrative than the meat industry, as it takes five years to pay for a cow and only six months to pay for a dog. The females end up in small confined spaces where males impregnate them; they then live in squalid, overcrowded wire cages, never stepping on grass, going for a walk, being washed or given medical attention when needed. They give birth typically 58-68 days later to a litter of puppies, which are quickly sold. The puppies are taken from their mother so early that many end up with psychological issues, not to mention how their mother must feel. The females are bred continuously until they are no longer physically capable, and then they are shot or otherwise disposed of. And there are kitten mills just like there are puppy mills. Most pet stores have no idea of the conditions the animals come from or are lied to, so when customers ask, they have a squeaky-clean reputation. Buying from pet stores doesn't guarantee that you are getting a healthy animal because puppies and kittens from mills have parasites, hidden genetic and health problems, and behavioral issues.[82]

Some mills notify animal shelters to collect females that are no longer able to give birth. Unfortunately, these notifications often come at short notice, sometimes as little as 45 minutes before their lives are ended. And it doesn't get much better for them when they reach the shelter. They are typically allowed 5-7 days to be adopted. If that doesn't happen, they are euthanized. That's not to say that all shelters kill unadopted animals. Some are strictly opposed to that ever happening to any of these beautiful beings, but they are a rarity. Most shelters are forced, because of space and budgetary constraints, to euthanize the animals in their care. And herein lies another problem. The most humane euthanasia is a lethal injection that painlessly stops the heart from beating, but it's expensive. Which means many shelters are forced to revert to methods like gas chambers (which can take half an hour to "work"), decompression chambers (animals are locked in small metal compartments that spin very fast and stop the animal from breathing, eventually causing death) and even electrocution (where the animal is made to bite onto a metal clip while a metal rectal electrocution probe is used)—methods which are inhumane, painful, and unacceptable.[83]

Did you know that approximately 1.5 million shelter animals are euthanized (670,000 dogs and 860,000 cats) each year in the US alone?[84] That raises the alarm that there is something seriously wrong with the system. This number used to be even higher! When we have an oversupply of domestic animals, the unwanted, stray or unadopted animals have no home and get put down because they have nowhere to go. Imagine if this is what happened to humans without a home. There would be a public outcry. All animals, domesticated or not, should have a fair chance at life. We need to collectively work out a way to reduce the oversupply that leads to such a high number of murdered animals every year.

And it doesn't stop with cats and dogs. Our desire to own exotic animals, often endangered species, means the illegal exotic pet trade is booming. Wild animals are ripped from their natural environment, thrown into tiny, overcrowded cages and shipped across the world, exposed to freezing cold and intolerably hot temperatures, inadequate food and water. Many die on route to their new homes, which are, no matter how much love we might surround them with, entirely incapable to meet these animals' behavioral, physical and social needs.[85] Just like unwanted cats and dogs, every year thousands of exotic animals end up on the street, with nowhere to go, in environmental conditions they are simply not equipped to deal with.[86]

So what can we do? Other than not supporting the exotic animal trade, if you're looking for a pet, your first stop should be an animal shelter. You might think that the dogs and cats you can adopt from a shelter are older, not purebred and have issues, but that isn't the case. Around 25% of dogs in shelters are purebred, and there's nothing wrong with getting an adult dog. What you see at the shelter is what you'll get at home. Puppies are much more unpredictable, and you don't know how their character will evolve when they grow up.

We need to raise our level of consciousness and treat every single being with as much respect as we would each other. We should put ourselves in their shoes: the amount of fear and uncertainty that many of these animals go through is unimaginable. You might argue that so do many humans, and yes, that is very true. But animals don't have a voice; we need to be that voice for them. We need to be a voice for everything that is unjust in this world. And we can start with our pets, our diet, and our lifestyle.

I LOVE ANIMALS BUT...

… But I could never give up (insert animal product here).

This is by far the most common excuse we hear when we talk to others about veganism. There's always something holding them back. Bacon, cheese, designer handbags.

Most humans love animals or at least appreciate their existence. And yes, a large percentage of us have pets and absolutely adore them. We don't like to think of anything wrong ever happening to them, rush them to the vet at the first hint of a problem, give them love, food, shelter, warmth.

The majority of people asked would balk in disgust if you suggested they eat a fillet of a cat, or a rib of dog, but can comfortably tuck into a chicken burger. Why is our compassion only ever awake when it comes to cats and dogs, or other animals deemed "cute" enough? A life is a life. Whether it's a pig, cat, cow, goat, dog or chicken—they all have the right to live free from fear, pain, and exploitation. We are so horrified by the dog meat industry in places like Indonesia and Korea, but it is no different to the industry that condemns billions of cows, pigs and hens to be raised and slaughtered for their meat.

When domestic animals are put into the same category as farmed animals, all of a sudden we don't have the mental capacity to deal with the truth of the pain and suffering we cause them. They are classified as different, and we can't envisage cats and dogs being treated the same way as cows.

We throw it into the "too hard" basket.

"I know there are billions of animals being slaughtered each year for human consumption, but I'd prefer not to think about it as I'm going through a tough time right now/I haven't got the answers/I'm too busy to change my lifestyle at the moment."

This is the story we tell ourselves. This is the story we told ourselves for 26 years! We're aware of the problem but, ultimately, we put ourselves and our needs before others. We put our convenience and our taste buds before the life of other sentient beings.

We could say no to leather and save animal lives, but we'd rather keep buying "high quality" leather bags and shoes because they are just too pretty not to buy. Besides, there aren't any alternatives that will last as long as leather, and fast fashion shoes fall apart after only one season. But we *do* have options: the vegan fashion industry is growing fast when it comes to alternatives for leather. Materials such as pinatex from pineapple, tree bark leather, cork, recycled tires, paper, recycled rubber, waxed cotton, apple fibers, MuSkin from mushrooms, and teak leaves are sustainable, cruelty-free options.[87]

We could go vegan and save animals lives, but we'd rather go to our favorite meat restaurant than change our habits. We'd rather do what everyone else is doing instead of risking our friends being uncomfortable with our decision. Besides, won't we feel entirely isolated when all the places we usually eat at don't have anything vegan on the menu? Have we bothered to ask the question though?

This all ties into how we interact socially. We'd rather go to the zoo to fit in with the people around us than make a stand by not supporting the industries that are causing animals harm. Not just entertainment; food and eating out are a big part of our social lives. What most people don't realize is that you *can* enjoy a social life while being vegan. Going away for a fishing weekend and eating at the local seafood restaurant is a good example: nothing is stopping you going on a boat trip, just don't catch any fish, and calling the restaurant ahead of time to check they can make something off-menu for you. There's an abundance of activities that don't revolve around food and will challenge you to explore more than you would otherwise. Food is an integral part of most cultures, but it doesn't have to be a barrier to your social life with family and friends.

We feel a special mention here should go to cheese, which seems to be the number one food would-be vegans simply can't give up. Well, there's a good reason you can't give it up: according to a study by the University of Michigan, cheese is as addictive as drugs.[88],[89] Its high-fat content triggers your brain to release dopamine, your very own pleasure chemical. Plus, the casein in cheese triggers the brain's opioid receptors, and these are linked to addiction. But good news: you don't have to give up cheese when you're vegan, you can switch to a non-addictive, healthier, nut-based version. Ten years ago, things were different, there was perhaps one vegan cheese on the market, and it tasted like chalk. But now you'll find at least ten brands of vegan cheese to choose from at most health food stores and even supermarkets. Or you can easily make your own with cashews. If there's a will, there's a way.

Often it comes down to convenience and what we deem as "a good time." We've learned to associate good times with food, usually meat-based (think about it, every single festive menu has several animal-derived dishes). But there's no tiptoeing around it, willingly ignoring the fact that living beings are losing their lives in a violent, cruel way just so we can eat a burger, is an act of selfishness. And unfortunately, while we may not like to admit it, many of us are comfortable being selfish. We don't want to think about it in that way, but when it's all laid out like this, what reason is left?

We all have it in us to change for the better. Whether or not we do is merely a matter of will. Isn't it time we put others first for a change? Isn't it time we put our health first? Changing our habits starts with a first step: the decision to make a positive difference. You can make that decision today.

A PLASTIC WORLD

Our modern society has been addicted to plastics since the 50s.[90] How many of us think about the daily choices we make around single-use plastics? Or plastic use in general? We have made more plastic in the last decade than we have in the previous century.[91] Half of it is disposable, which means it's created to be used once only and then tossed away. To date, over 8.3 billion metric tons of plastic have been made.[92] Have you ever wondered where that plastic goes? Think about this: almost every single piece of plastic ever made still exists somewhere today.

You may be wondering what plastic has to do with veganism and animal welfare? A lot, actually. Did you know that about eight million tons of plastic are dumped into our oceans every single year? Around 70% of this plastic ends up floating to the bottom.[93] Some of it looks like fish food. Not knowing how to differentiate between a plastic bag and a jellyfish condemns many sea animals to a painful death. Over time, the sun's ultraviolet light, waves and sea salt break down the plastics into micro-beads. These tiny particles typically create a plastic smog over the surface of the ocean. Sea life ends up eating the plastic, filling their little bodies with something that can't pass through them. Bigger fish then eat little fish, so the cycle of plastic continues to be passed onto almost all marine life. Plastic has no nutritional value whatsoever. Worse, it's highly toxic. Those toxins leach into muscles and fat, causing the fish pain.[94],[95] If you still eat seafood, you are ingesting the plastic chemicals that they have absorbed into their bodies.[96]

And plastic affects more than the delicate balance of the marine food chain. Animals are caught in old fishing nets that have been dumped overboard; plastic rings strangle animals like seals and turtles. We've all seen the photos of the devastating effects of plastic on our ocean life, but our habits have not shifted fast enough to save these beautiful creatures.

It isn't just fish that suffer, but birds too. They go out to find food for their chicks and come back with plastic that they found floating in the ocean thinking it is food. Scientists who have studied these birds have found various pieces of plastic in their stomachs, sometimes so large that you wonder how they ever swallowed them. Some 90% of all seabirds have ingested plastic at some point in their lives.[97] Many also die from it filling their stomach to the point where they can no longer eat. We keep babies safe by keeping small easily ingestible bits of plastic away from them. We need to have the same consideration for animals, especially when these animals are suffering because of something they have not done themselves. They never created an un-biodegradable, toxic product from fossil fuels. We did. And we need to take responsibility, find a solution and stop putting them in danger.

Our oceans are overfished and overburdened with toxic chemicals and rubbish. Unfortunately, if we keep producing and throwing away plastic at this rate, and if our garbage management practices don't evolve, it's estimated that by 2025, the amount of plastic dumped into the sea will reach a staggering 155 million tons a year.[98] We've already got one plastic island in the Pacific Ocean, do we want a second? A third?[99],[100] Even islands that are uninhabited by humans are now littered with plastic debris.[101] And plastic doesn't break down but breaks up: it's here to stay. We have no way of filtering the whole ocean to remove all the toxic rubbish we're dumping into it.

And it's not only the plastic that we toss out or leave behind that's causing the issues. Everything that we flush down the drain mostly ends up in our oceans too. Micro-beads, found in facial exfoliators, toothpaste and other cosmetics, add to the mountain of plastics that end up in the oceans today.[102] In countries like the US, Ireland, and the Netherlands, micro-beads are slowly being banned in products. You still need to be vigilant to ensure you're not buying a product with plastic particles that will get flushed down the drain.[103]

It's worth noting here that plastic doesn't just harm the fish and the ocean, it damages our bodies as well. Plastics contain endocrine disrupting chemicals. These are chemicals that mimic hormones in the body, and end up causing a host of health complications, from infertility to cancer. They affect your reproductive, nervous and immune systems. What's more, they also create developmental problems, so pregnant women need to be especially mindful to avoid them.[104],[105] When we carelessly toss these into the ocean, when we use plastic containers to cook or store our food or water, we're exposing ourselves to these endocrine disrupters. We're polluting and harming our bodies at the same time as polluting the oceans and harming animals.

We deserve better, the animals deserve better and so does our planet. Our mentality needs to shift from "this is someone else's problem" to "we are all in this together." We can't afford to carry on with our crazy consuming and think that change will come from other people. Change needs to start with us. Every single one of us has a part to play. Every single bit matters. We certainly hope that by 2050, when the human population is predicted to reach 10 billion, plastic production hasn't tripled as forecasted![106]

If we want to reduce the amount of plastic waste we create, we need to focus on the concept of zero waste. This idea aligns beautifully with our minimalist mindset, and it begs the questions: what are you bringing into your household, and what is the lifespan of that item? If the sole purpose of the item was to bring your dinner from point A to point B one night, then this is single-use, and you should consider an alternative. However, if it's something that you use every single day and it just so happens to be plastic that you've had for a long time, and you're not putting food or liquid in it, then carry on.

Just like any addiction, there comes a point when we must learn to say no. Having recognized the environmental and physical damage that plastics are responsible for, we now need to move away from them. The idea is to reduce as much as possible the addition of any new plastics to our lives, especially single-use ones which can in many cases be avoided if we are prepared and conscious of our choices. For example, you can bring your own (metal) straw or cutlery when drinking or eating take out. You can take reusable bags when you're shopping or even keep spare containers in your car in case you need to take home leftovers. When we start to shift our mindset around these simple but easily overseen situations, we can make a difference. These actions, in turn, send a message to shops, restaurants, cafes and business owners that plastic should be a thing of the past and more sustainable alternatives need to be implemented.

When you have a strong 'why', the 'how' becomes much easier. It doesn't take much to do some research, go through your cupboards and start choosing alternatives today that help you be healthier, protect the animals, and support the planet.

THE MINIMALIST VEGAN

There has never been a better moment in history to take a stand. While our world is rocked by conflict, environmental crises, and economic instability, we can all play a role in bringing peace and love to the world through our actions.

Being an activist doesn't have to mean standing, balaclava-clad, shouting and throwing bricks at shop windows that sell non-vegan products. You can be an activist for peace, an activist for the animals, an activist for the planet every single day, through the choices you make and the brands you support.

By turning away from "The More Virus" of rampant consumerism, you can reconnect with what really matters in your life—family, friends, joyful experiences, connection. By turning your back on meat and animal by-products, you can help end animal cruelty and create a sustainable future. By being a voice of peace and love, you create more peace and love in the world.

GRATITUDE

We believe an attitude of gratitude brings true happiness. And when you're making changes that could be uncomfortable, gratitude is your best friend.

As you transition to minimalism and veganism, there may be days when you find it hard. Your family questions your motives, and your friends pick a steakhouse for your catch-up, your cupboards may be so full of "essentials" you despair of ever making space. When you notice yourself getting angry, or frustrated, or upset, stop. And come back to gratitude. There's always something to feel grateful for.

Take a deep breath and mentally list three things you're grateful for right that second. It could be the warmth of a ray of sun on your skin, a smile from your loving partner, having running water, sharing a coffee break with your best friend. Feeling grateful for what you do have in your life right now, rather than focusing on what is wrong, is a powerful practice that will bring you back to the present, back to mindfulness, and back to a state of contentment. And from this state of peace, it becomes easy to make positive changes.

So here we'd like to take the opportunity to give gratitude to some special people who made this journey possible.

Family

Even though our values don't always align, your support and acceptance have meant the world to us. Thank you for helping us create original recipes, workshop examples and provide endless experiences that have shaped who we are today. And to our parents, thank you for giving us the gift of life.

Seth Godin

Your commitment to teaching the importance of being authentic and standing for something has had a larger impact than you know. You've shown us that connection and realness are what matter and that we can all make a difference using our voice.

Leo Babauta

We are so grateful to have stumbled across your blog many years ago. It was your humble and honest writing that inspired us to live a minimalist, vegan lifestyle. Thank you for your support over the years and thanks for taking the time to show us around San Francisco. You're just as generous and inspiring in person as you are online.

Rich Roll

You have provided hours upon hours of inspiration and knowledge through your podcast. After listening to you for so long, we feel like we know you personally. Thank you for putting out such fantastic content with amazing guests. Our walks and time spent in the kitchen have become our favorite parts of the day thanks to you.

Fizzle.Co

Corbett, Chase, Caleb, Barret, and Steph. You guys really do help indie entrepreneurs make a living doing something that they care about. It's through your content and community that we've learned how to share our message with tens of thousands of people each month. Thank you for your advice and endless laughs.

Prem Rawat

Thank you for your wise words and message. Every time we hear you speak, it helps us to reconnect with ourselves and remember to be grateful for each breath. You have truly given us the meaning of life.

Readers

You, reader, are the reason we started The Minimalist Vegan and why we've written this book. Your passion, emails, and comments keep us connected to our message. Thank you for taking the time out of your day to read and share our content. And double thanks to those of you who have taken action to live a minimalist, vegan lifestyle. We're grateful you've made this step and excited to be part of your journey.

ABOUT THE AUTHORS

We're Maša and Michael Ofei, a married couple from Canberra, Australia with a passion for simple, compassionate living.

Maša loves the simple things in life. She's a certified health coach, or "the health nerd" and professional photographer. One of her favorite things to do is shopping at farmers markets, local bulk stores and finding the best organic foods, and transforming them into tasty vegan dishes.

Michael believes there should be more minimalist, vegan men in this world. He's passionate about stripping things back to the essentials and finding the most efficient way of doing things to spend more time enjoying life. You'll see him connecting and networking with like-minded people and writing articles on simple living.

To take you back to the beginning of our journey, when we first heard about minimalism, we pictured someone in linen clothes, sitting in a dull white room surrounded by nothing. But as we learned more about it from people like Leo Babauta, we realized that minimalism could be the perfect cure for what we call "The More Virus": the mentality of always wanting more.

We weren't always minimalists. We used to take on many different commitments and spread ourselves too thin. We wanted to work up the corporate ladder, buy multiple houses, have beautiful clothes and cars. Minimalism enabled us to see that there was a different way to define success and helped us turn away from what is (directly or indirectly) advertised to us. Minimalism gave us the confidence to effectively quit things that weren't adding real value to our lives, whether it was dead-end jobs, things we owned but didn't need, businesses we were no longer passionate about, or negative friends.

All of a sudden, success wasn't about material things anymore. It was about having simple, enriching experiences on our own terms.

Our journey towards veganism was similar to what many new vegans experience. We gathered up the courage to watch the documentary Earthlings one evening and became vegan overnight. In fact, Michael was eating a chicken kebab earlier that day! For us, it was impossible to go back to consuming animals and their by-products after making the connection.

Both lifestyles have drastically heightened our awareness and have enriched our lives in ways we previously thought weren't possible.

That's ultimately how we came up with the concept for our blog (and later this book), The Minimalist

Vegan. Our goal is to live with compassion and simplicity each and every day and empower people to think more mindfully about what they consume.

NOTES

[1] Brooke, Z. (2017). *Digital Ad Spending Expected to Near $250 Billion by 2019*. [online] Ama.org. Available at: https://www.ama.org/publications/eNewsletters/Marketing-News-Weekly/Pages/report-250-billion-digital-ad-spend-2019.aspx.

[2] ScienceDaily. (2008). *Decision-making May Be Surprisingly Unconscious Activity*. [online] Available at: https://www.sciencedaily.com/releases/2008/04/080414145705.htm.

[3] Psychologistworld.com. (n.d.). *Can Subliminal Messages In Adverts Influence Our Behavior?*. [online] Available at: https://www.psychologistworld.com/influence-personality/subliminal-advertising.

[4] Mag.ispo.com. (2015). *90 Percent Of All Purchasing Decisions Are Made Subconsciously - ISPO News – Magazin*. [online] Available at: http://mag.ispo.com/2015/01/90-percent-of-all-purchasing-decisions-are-made-subconsciously/?lang=en.

[5] ScienceDaily. (2008). *Decision-making May Be Surprisingly Unconscious Activity.* [online] Available at: https://www.sciencedaily.com/releases/2008/04/080414145705.htm.

[6] Students.arch.utah.edu. [online] Available at: http://students.arch.utah.edu/courses/Arch4011/Recycling%20-Facts1.pdf.

[7] SpaceX. (2017). *Mars.* [online] Available at: http://www.spacex.com/mars.

[8] Frazee, G. (2016). *How to stop 13 million tons of clothing from getting trashed every year.* [online] PBS NewsHour. Available at: https://www.pbs.org/newshour/nation/how-to-stop-13-million-tons-of-clothing-from-getting-trashed-every-year.

[9] SMARTASN. (n.d.). *Frequently Asked Questions.* [online] Available at: https://www.smartasn.org/resources/frequently-asked-questions/.

[10] Lyday, E. (2014). *How Many Pounds of Textiles Are Trashed Every Year? [Infographic] | Daily Infographic.* [online] Dailyinfographic.com. Available at: http://www.dailyinfographic.com/how-many-pounds-of-textiles-are-trashed-every-year.

11 Sweeny, G. (2015). *Fast Fashion Is the Second Dirtiest Industry in the World, Next to Big Oil.* [online] EcoWatch. Available at: https://www.ecowatch.com/fast-fashion-is-the-second-dirtiest-industry-in-the-world-next-to-big--1882083445.html.

12 Michael, P. (2011). *The Psychology of Free, and Its Power Over You.* [online] Wise Bread. Available at: http://www.wisebread.com/the-psychology-of-free-and-its-power-over-you.

13 Oxford Dictionaries | English. (n.d.). *compassion | Definition of compassion in English by Oxford Dictionaries.* [online] Available at: https://en.oxforddictionaries.com/definition/compassion.

14 Safina, C. (2017). *Elephants mourn. Dogs love. Why do we deny the feelings of other species?.* [online] the Guardian. Available at: https://www.theguardian.com/environment/2017/oct/11/elephants-animal-welfare-why-do-we-deny-ignore-feelings-other-species.

[15] Hunt, E. (2017). *Meatonomics author says government working with meat and dairy industry to boost consumption.* [online] the Guardian. Available at: https://www.theguardian.com/science/2017/may/06/meatonomics-author-says-government-working-with-meat-and-dairy-industry-to-boost-consumption.

[16] COWSPIRACY. (n.d.). *Facts and Sources.* [online] Available at: http://www.cowspiracy.com/facts/.

[17] Simon, D. (2014). *It's Time to Stop Pretending Organic, Grass-Fed Etc Animal Products Are Sustainable & Eco-Friendly.* [online] Free From Harm. Available at: https://freefromharm.org/agriculture-environment/organic-meat-not-sustainable/.

[18] Yang, S. (2006). *Pollinators help one-third of world's crop production, says new study.* [online] Berkeley.edu. Available at: https://berkeley.edu/news/media/releases/2006/10/25_pollinator.shtml.

[19] Weisman, A. (2005). *Earth Without People | DiscoverMagazine.com.* [online] Discover Magazine. Available at: http://discovermagazine.com/2005/feb/earth-without-people.

[20] COWSPIRACY. (n.d.). *Facts and Sources*. [online] Available at: http://www.cowspiracy.com/facts/.

[21] Hyner, C. (2015). *A Leading Cause of Everything: One Industry That Is Destroying Our Planet and Our Ability to Thrive on It Georgetown Environmental Law Review*. [online] Georgetown Environmental Law Review. Available at: https://gelr.org/2015/10/23/a-leading-cause-of-everything-one-industry-that-is-destroying-our-planet-and-our-ability-to-thrive-on-it-georgetown-environmental-law-review/.

[22] COWSPIRACY. (n.d.). *Facts and Sources*. [online] Available at: http://www.cowspiracy.com/facts/.

[23] Parker, L. (2016). *What You Need to Know About the World's Water Wars*. [online] News.nationalgeographic.com. Available at: https://news.nationalgeographic.com/2016/07/world-aquifers-water-wars/.

[24] Goldenberg, S. (2014). *Why global water shortages pose threat of terror and war*. [online] the Guardian. Available at: https://www.theguardian.com/environment/2014/feb/09/global-water-shortages-threat-terror-war.

25 Barber, N. (2009). *Summary of Estimated Water Use in the United States in 2005*. [online] Pubs.usgs.gov. Available at: https://pubs.usgs.gov/fs/2009/3098/pdf/2009-3098.pdf.

26 Geetanjali*, C., Akashdeep,, D., Subham, A. and Keka, O. (2015). *Hydraulic Fracturing for Oil and Gas and its Environmental Impacts*. [online] Isca.in. Available at: http://www.isca.in/rjrs/archive/v4/iISC-2014/1.ISCA-ISC-2014-Oral-8EVS-24.pdf.

27 COWSPIRACY. (2017). *Facts and Sources*. [online] Available at: http://www.cowspiracy.com/facts.

28 Roach, J. (2006). *Seafood May Be Gone by 2048, Study Says*. [online] News.nationalgeographic.com. Available at: https://news.nationalgeographic.com/news/2006/11/061102-seafood-threat.html.

29 Cave, D. and Gillis, J. (2017). *Large Sections of Australia's Great Reef Are Now Dead, Scientists Find*. [online] Nytimes.com. Available at: https://www.nytimes.com/2017/03/15/science/great-barrier-reef-coral-climate-change-dieoff.html.

[30] Thornton, P., Herrero, M. and Ericksen, P. (2011). *Livestock and climate change*. [online] Cgspace.cgiar.org. Available at: https://cgspace.cgiar.org/bitstream/handle/10568/10601/IssueBrief3.pdf.

[31] Roach, J. (2006). *Seafood May Be Gone by 2048, Study Says*. [online] News.nationalgeographic.com. Available at: https://news.nationalgeographic.com/news/2006/11/061102-seafood-threat.html.

[32] Sarma, P. (2014). *Beef Production is Killing the Amazon Rainforest*. [online] One Green Planet. Available at: http://www.onegreenplanet.org/animalsandnature/beef-production-is-killing-the-amazon-rainforest/.

[33] Scientific American. (n.d.). *Measuring the Daily Destruction of the World's Rainforests*. [online] Available at: https://www.scientificamerican.com/article/earth-talks-daily-destruction/.

[34] Nrcs.usda.gov. (1995). *Animal Manure Management*. [online] Available at: https://www.nrcs.usda.gov/wps/portal/nrcs/detail/null/?cid=nrcs143_014211.

35 Extension2.missouri.edu. (n.d.). Assessing the Risk of Groundwater Contamination From Animal Manure Management Facilities. [online] Available at: https://extension2.missouri.edu/WQ657.

36 Macklin, M. (2017). *Animal Agriculture – Killing More than Just Cows. How Farm Run-Off Threatens Marine Life.* [online] One Green Planet. Available at: http://www.onegreenplanet.org/environment/how-factory-farm-run-off-threatens-marine-life/.

37 Fox News. (2008). *Study Finds Traces of Drugs in Drinking Water in 24 Major U.S. Regions.* [online] Available at: http://www.foxnews.com/story/2008/03/10/study-finds-traces-drugs-in-drinking-water-in-24-major-us-regions.html.

38 Vaidyanathan, G. (2015). *How Bad of a Greenhouse Gas Is Methane?.* [online] Scientific American. Available at: https://www.scientificamerican.com/article/how-bad-of-a-greenhouse-gas-is-methane/.

[39] Goodland, R. and Anhang, J. (2009). *Livestock and Climate Change*. [online] Worldwatch.org. Available at: http://www.worldwatch.org/files/pdf/Livestock%20and%20-Climate%20Change.pdf.

[40] Hickman, M. (2009). *Study claims meat creates half of all greenhouse gases*. [online] The Independent. Available at: http://www.independent.co.uk/environment/climate-change/study-claims-meat-creates-half-of-all-greenhouse-gases-1812909.html.

[41] Margulis, S. (2004). *Causes of Deforestation of the Brazilian Amazon*. [online] Documents.worldbank.org. Available at: http://documents.worldbank.org/curated/en/758171468768828889/pdf/277150PAPER0wbw-p0no1022.pdf.

[42] Human Rights Watch. (n.d.). *Meatpacking's Human Toll*. [online] Available at: https://www.hrw.org/news/2005/08/02/meatpackings-human-toll.

[43] Greenhouse, S. (2005). *CorpWatch : US: Meat Packing Industry Criticized on Human Rights Grounds*. [online] Corp-watch.org. Available at: http://www.corpwatch.org/article.php?id=11806.

[44] Schlosser, E. (2001). Fast Food Nation: The Dark Side of the All-American Meal. New York: Houghton Mifflin Company

[45] Oxford Dictionaries | English. (n.d.). *speciesism | Definition of speciesism in English by Oxford Dictionaries.* [online] Available at: https://en.oxforddictionaries.com/definition/speciesism.

[46] Skutch A. 1996. The Minds of Birds.College Station (TX): Texas A&M University Press; Poole J. 1996. Coming of Age With Elephants: A Memoir. New York: Hyperion.; Panksepp J. 1998. Affective Neuroscience. New York: Oxford University Press.; Archer J. 1999. The Nature of Grief: The Evolution and Psychology of Reactions to Loss. New York: Routledge.; Cabanac M. 1999. Emotion and phylogeny. Journal of Consciousness Studies, p176–190.; Bekoff M. 2000. The Smile of a Dolphin: Remarkable Accounts of Animal Emotions. New York: Random House/Discovery Books.

[47] Low, P. (2012). *The Cambridge Declaration on Consciousness.* [online] Fcmconference.org. Available at: http://fcmconference.org/img/CambridgeDeclarationOnConsciousness.pdf.

[48] Fawec.org. (n.d.). *Tail biting in pigs.* [online] Available at: https://www.fawec.org/en/fact-sheets/36-swine/114-tail-biting-in-pigs.

[49] HuffPost. (2011). *Video Shows Chicks Ground Up Alive.* [online] Available at: https://www.huffingtonpost.com/2009/09/01/chicks-being-ground-up-al_n_273652.html.

[50] Humanesociety.org. (n.d.). *Circus Myths : The Humane Society of the United States.* [online] Available at: http://www.humanesociety.org/issues/circuses_entertainment/facts/circus_myths.html.

[51] Blackfish. (2017). *Blackfish.* [online] Available at: http://www.blackfishmovie.com/.

52 Skutch A. 1996. The Minds of Birds.College Station (TX): Texas A&M University Press; Poole J. 1996. Coming of Age With Elephants: A Memoir. New York: Hyperion.; Panksepp J. 1998. Affective Neuroscience. New York: Oxford University Press.; Archer J. 1999. The Nature of Grief: The Evolution and Psychology of Reactions to Loss. New York: Routledge.; Cabanac M. 1999. Emotion and phylogeny. Journal of Consciousness Studies, p176–190.; Bekoff M. 2000. The Smile of a Dolphin: Remarkable Accounts of Animal Emotions. New York: Random House/Discovery Books.

53 Low, P. (2012). *The Cambridge Declaration on Consciousness*. [online] Fcmconference.org. Available at: http://fcmconference.org/img/CambridgeDeclarationOnConsciousness.pdf.

54 Low, P. (2012). *The Cambridge Declaration on Consciousness*. [online] Fcmconference.org. Available at: http://fcmconference.org/img/CambridgeDeclarationOnConsciousness.pdf.

[55] PETA. (n.d.). *Animals Used for Experimentation*. [online] Available at: https://www.peta.org/issues/animals-used-for-experimentation/.

[56] PETA. (n.d.). *Mice and Rats in Laboratories*. [online] Available at: https://www.peta.org/issues/animals-used-for-experimentation/animals-laboratories/mice-rats-laboratories/.

[57] PETA. (n.d.). *These Companies Test on Animals. Which Brands Made The List?*. [online] Available at: https://www.peta.org/living/beauty/companies-test-on-animals/.

[58] Geer, A. (2013). *7 Shocking Products You Wouldn't Believe Are Tested on Animals*. [online] Care2 Causes. Available at: http://www.care2.com/causes/7-shocking-products-you-wouldnt-believe-are-tested-on-animals.html.

[59] LLC, S. (2017). *Cruelty-Free on the App Store*. [online] App Store. Available at: https://itunes.apple.com/us/app/cruelty-free/id313825734?mt=8.

[60] CCF Official Site. (2017). *The CCF App*. [online] Available at: http://www.choosecrueltyfree.org.au/the-ccf-app/.

[61] Crueltyfreeinternational.org. (n.d.). *Types of animal testing | Cruelty Free International.* [online] Available at: https://www.crueltyfreeinternational.org/why-we-do-it/types-animal-testing.

[62] Crueltyfreeinternational.org. (n.d.). *Types of animal testing | Cruelty Free International.* [online] Available at: https://www.crueltyfreeinternational.org/why-we-do-it/types-animal-testing.

[63] Anand, P., Kunnumakara, A., Sundaram, C., Harikumar, K., Tharakan, S., Lai, O., Sung, B. and Aggarwal, B. (2008). *Cancer is a Preventable Disease that Requires Major Lifestyle Changes.* [online] ncbi.nlm.nih.gov. Available at: https://www.ncbi.nlm.nih.gov/pmc/articles/PMC2515569/.

[64] Willett, W., Koplan, J., Nugent, R., Dusenbury, C., Puska, P. and Gaziano, T. (2006). *Prevention of Chronic Disease by Means of Diet and Lifestyle Changes.* [online] Ncbi.nlm.nih.gov. Available at: https://www.ncbi.nlm.nih.gov/books/NBK11795/.

[65] ScienceDaily. (2011). *How many species on Earth? About 8.7 million, new estimate says.* [online] Available at: https://www.sciencedaily.com/releases/2011/08/110823180459.htm.

[66] Ofei, M. (2015). *What's Up With The Fashion Industry?.* [online] The Minimalist Vegan. Available at: https://theminimalistvegan.com/fashion-industry/#more-1431.

[67] War On Want. (n.d.). *Sweatshops in Bangladesh.* [online] Available at: https://waronwant.org/sweatshops-bangladesh.

[68] Human Rights Watch. (2012). *Toxic Tanneries | The Health Repercussions of Bangladesh's Hazaribagh Leather.* [online] Available at: https://www.hrw.org/report/2012/10/08/toxic-tanneries/health-repercussions-bangladeshs-hazaribagh-leather.

[69] PETA. (n.d.). *The Leather Industry.* [online] Available at: https://www.peta.org/issues/animals-used-for-clothing/leather-industry/.

70 Action.peta.org.uk. (n.d.). *Shocking Undercover Investigation: Dogs Bludgeoned and Killed for Leather.* [online] Available at: http://action.peta.org.uk/ea-action/action?ea.client.id=5&ea.campaign.id=32963.

71 Lennon, C. (2013). *Leather Is More Than "a By-Product of the Meat Industry".* [online] One Green Planet. Available at: http://www.onegreenplanet.org/animalsandnature/leather-is-more-than-a-by-product-of-the-meat-industry/.

72 PETA. (n.d.). *Inside the Wool Industry.* [online] Available at: https://www.peta.org/issues/animals-used-for-clothing/animals-used-clothing-factsheets/inside-wool-industry/.

73 PETA. (n.d.). *The Fur Industry: Animals Used for Their Skins.* [online] Available at: https://www.peta.org/issues/animals-used-for-clothing/fur/.

74 Rutherford-Fortunati, A. (2013). *How Down Feathers are Collected.* [online] Gentleworld.org. Available at: http://gentleworld.org/how-down-feathers-are-collected/.

[75] Wwf.panda.org. (n.d.). *Cotton: a water wasting crop.* [online] Available at: http://wwf.panda.org/about_our_earth/about_freshwater/freshwater_problems/thirsty_crops/cotton/.

[76] Brandford, S. (2008). *Indian farmers shun GM for organic solutions.* [online] the Guardian. Available at: https://www.theguardian.com/environment/2008/jul/30/gm-crops.india.

[77] Cummins, R. (2017). *Beyond Monsanto's GMO Cotton: Why Consumers Need to Care What We Wear.* [online] Organicconsumers.org. Available at: https://www.organic-consumers.org/essays/beyond-monsantos-gmo-cotton-why-consumers-need-care-what-we-wear.

[78] Iarc.fr. (2015). *IARC Monographs Volume 112: evaluation of five organophosphate insecticides and herbicides.* [online] Available at: https://www.iarc.fr/en/media-centre/iarcnews/pdf/MonographVolume112.pdf

[79] WebMD. (n.d.). *Endocrine Disorders: Types, Causes, Symptoms, and Treatments.* [online] Available at: https://www.webmd.com/diabetes/endocrine-system-disorders#1.

[80] Cummins, R. (2017). *Beyond Monsanto's GMO Cotton: Why Consumers Need to Care What We Wear.* [online] Organicconsumers.org. Available at: https://www.organic-consumers.org/essays/beyond-monsantos-gmo-cotton-why-consumers-need-care-what-we-wear.

[81] Mensah, P., Palmer, C. and Odume, O. (2015). *Ecotoxicology of Glyphosate and Glyphosate-Based Herbicides — Toxicity to Wildlife and Humans.* [online] Intechopen.com. Available at: https://www.intechopen.com/books/toxicity-and-hazard-of-agrochemicals/ecotoxicology-of-glyphosate-and-glyphosate-based-herbicides-toxicity-to-wildlife-and-humans.

[82] ASPCA. (n.d.). *Puppy Mills.* [online] Available at: https://www.aspca.org/animal-cruelty/puppy-mills.

[83] Animal-pounds.com. (n.d.). *HOW PETS ARE KILLED IN POUNDS AND SHELTERS.* [online] Available at: http://www.animal-pounds.com/how_are_pets_killed_in_pounds_and_shelters.html.

[84] ASPCA. (n.d.). *Pet Statistics.* [online] Available at: https://www.aspca.org/animal-homelessness/shelter-intake-and-surrender/pet-statistics.

[85] Bornfreeusa.org. (2003). *The Dirty Side of the Exotic Animal Pet Trade.* [online] Available at: http://www.bornfreeusa.org/articles.php?more=1&p=180.

[86] Bornfreeusa.org. (n.d.). *Ten Fast Facts about Exotic "Pets".* [online] Available at: http://www.bornfreeusa.org/facts.php?p=439&more=1.

[87] Boscio, C. (n.d.). *12 Truly Eco Friendly Vegan Leathers - Eluxe Magazine.* [online] Eluxe Magazine. Available at: https://eluxemagazine.com/fashion/5-truly-eco-friendly-vegan-leathers/.

[88] Schulte, E., Avena, N. and Gearhardt, A. (2015). *Which Foods May Be Addictive? The Roles of Processing, Fat Content, and Glycemic Load.* [online] Plos.org. Available at: http://journals.plos.org/plosone/article?id=10.1371/journal.pone.0117959.

[89] Harris, J. (2015). *Cheese really is crack. Study reveals cheese is as addictive as drugs.* [online] latimes.com. Available at: http://www.latimes.com/food/dailydish/la-dd-cheese-addictive-drugs-20151022-story.html.

[90] Schlossberg, T. (2017). *The Immense, Eternal Footprint Humanity Leaves on Earth: Plastics.* [online] Nytimes.com. Available at: https://www.nytimes.com/2017/07/19/climate/plastic-pollution-study-science-advances.html.

[91] Zhang, S. (2017). *Half of All Plastic That Has Ever Existed Was Made in the Past 13 Years.* [online] The Atlantic. Available at: https://www.theatlantic.com/science/archive/2017/07/plastic-age/533955/.

[92] Schlossberg, T. (2017). *The Immense, Eternal Footprint Humanity Leaves on Earth: Plastics.* [online] Nytimes.com. Available at: https://www.nytimes.com/2017/07/19/climate/plastic-pollution-study-science-advances.html.

[93] Plastic Oceans Foundation. (2017). *Facts . About Plastic . Help - Plastic Oceans Foundation.* [online] Available at: https://www.plasticoceans.org/the-facts/.

[94] Biologicaldiversity.org. (n.d.). *Ocean Plastics Pollution.* [online] Available at: http://www.biologicaldiversity.org/campaigns/ocean_plastics/.

[95] Clean Water Action. (n.d.). *The Problem of Marine Plastic Pollution.* [online] Available at: https://www.cleanwater.org/problem-marine-plastic-pollution.

[96] Plastic Oceans Foundation. (2017). *Rethink Plastic. Save Our Seas • Plastic Oceans Foundation.* [online] Available at: https://www.plasticoceans.org/.

[97] Parker, L. (2015). *Nearly Every Seabird on Earth Is Eating Plastic.* [online] News.nationalgeographic.com. Available at: https://news.nationalgeographic.com/2015/09/15092-plastic-seabirds-albatross-australia/.

[98] Parker, L. (2015). *Eight Million Tons of Plastic Dumped in Ocean Every Year.* [online] News.nationalgeographic.com. Available at: https://news.nationalgeographic.com/news/2015/02/150212-ocean-debris-plastic-garbage-patches-science/.

[99] Garza, M. (2017). *Oh, great — another plastic garbage patch in the Pacific Ocean – LA Times.* [online] latimes.com. Available at: http://beta.latimes.com/opinion/opinion-la/la-ol-another-pacific-plastic-patch-20170720-story.html.

[100] En.wikipedia.org. (n.d.). *Great Pacific garbage patch.* [online] Available at: https://en.wikipedia.org/wiki/Great_Pacific_garbage_patch.

[101] Hunt, E. (2017). *38 million pieces of plastic waste found on uninhabited South Pacific island*. [online] the Guardian. Available at: https://www.theguardian.com/environment/2017/may/15/38-million-pieces-of-plastic-waste-found-on-uninhabited-south-pacific-island.

[102] Thorogood, I. (2016). *What are microbeads and why should we ban them? | Greenpeace UK*. [online] Greenpeace UK. Available at: https://www.greenpeace.org.uk/what-are-plastic-microbeads-and-why-should-we-ban-them-20160114/.

[103] Marsden, H. (2016). *These are the only countries that have banned harmful microbeads*. [online] indy100. Available at: https://www.indy100.com/article/microbeads-harmful-where-are-they-banned-countries-7549811.

[104] Yang, C., Yaniger, S., Jordan, V., Klein, D. and Bittner, G. (2011). *Most Plastic Products Release Estrogenic Chemicals: A Potential Health Problem That Can Be Solved*. [online] ncbi.nlm.nih.gov. Available at: https://www.ncbi.nlm.nih.gov/pmc/articles/PMC3222987/.

[105] Ecologycenter.org. (n.d.). *Adverse Health Effects of Plastics | Ecology Center.* [online] Available at: https://ecology-center.org/factsheets/adverse-health-effects-of-plastics/.

[106] Plastic Oceans Foundation. (2017). *Facts . About Plastic . Help - Plastic Oceans Foundation.* [online] Available at: https://www.plasticoceans.org/the-facts/.

Made in the USA
Monee, IL
03 December 2019